BUILDING A

Mobile App: Design and Program Your Own App!

by Sarah Guthals, Ph.D.

WILEY

20 Select Recording and drag a Call Recording.Play block into your When Play.Click block.

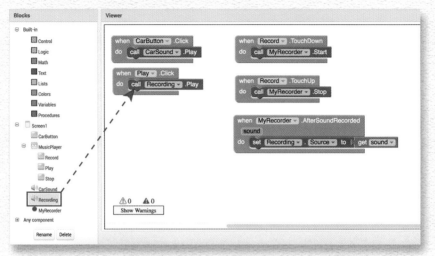

21 In the Blocks column, select Stop and drag a When Stop.Click block into your viewer, then select Recording and drag a Call Recording.Stop block into your When Stop.Click block.

10 Change the properties for both HorizontalArrangement items so that each has "Center:3" for AlignHorizontal and "Fill Parent" for Width.

Congratulations! You have your app all planned out!

4 Go back to your app on http://ai2.appinventor.mit.edu/ and click AI Companion.

4 Add the items: Under each item in the Components section on the left you will find a green block with the name of the item, like "Food1" at the bottom of the list of blocks that you can use. Drag and attach those food blocks (Food 1 through Food 10) to the Items openings on our Add Items block.

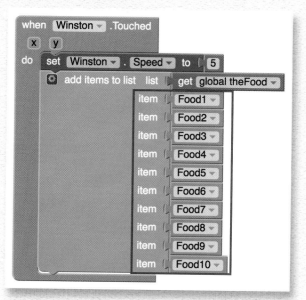

5 Change your collide block: Remove the = blocks and Set Visible blocks from your If Then Else block. Then, remove the Else part by clicking the blue button on the If Then block and dragging the Else out. Then, from Lists, drag an Is in List? block and attach it to your If Then block.

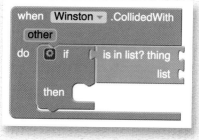